The Repair Guide For Iphone Microphone *For Seniors*

A Comprehensive Step-by-Step Method to Troubleshoot, Clean, and Fix Microphone Issues on your Phone

Gregory T. Scott

Disclaimer

Please be informed that this book is an unofficial Work. It does not in any way replace the original work or publication of Any Iphone Material. I recommend you make an index finding yourself online and follow pages for further information regarding current status or News Updates.

Contents

Introduction

Welcome to the DIY Guide to iPhone Microphone Repairs! The purpose of this guide is to help you understand and fix any issues you may encounter with your iPhone's microphones. Whether your microphone isn't working during phone calls, in apps, or while recording videos, this guide will provide you with step-by-step instructions to diagnose and resolve these problems.

Having a functional microphone is crucial for many of the features we rely on every day. When the microphone stops working, it can be very frustrating and limit your ability to use your phone effectively. This guide aims to empower you to solve these problems on your own, saving you time and money by avoiding unnecessary trips to a repair shop.

To effectively repair your iPhone's microphone, it is important to first understand how they work and where they are located. iPhones are equipped with multiple microphones, each serving a specific purpose to ensure high-quality sound for different functions.

Your iPhone typically has three microphones: the primary microphone, the front microphone, and the back microphone. The primary microphone is located at the bottom of the iPhone near the charging port. It is primarily used for phone calls and voice recordings. The front microphone is located near the front-facing camera and is used during FaceTime calls and when recording videos with the front camera.

The back microphone is near the rear camera and is used when recording videos with the back camera.

Each of these microphones has a specific role, and knowing their locations and functions will help you troubleshoot which microphone might be causing the problem.

Microphones in your iPhone convert sound waves into electrical signals that the phone can process. When you speak, the sound waves enter the microphone through small openings on your iPhone. Inside the microphone, a diaphragm vibrates with the sound waves, creating electrical signals that are then processed by the phone. If your microphone isn't working, it could be due to a blockage, a software issue, or a hardware problem. Blockages can occur if dirt, dust, or debris cover the microphone openings. Software issues might involve settings that need adjustment or apps that do not have permission to use the microphone. Hardware problems might involve damage to the microphone itself.

Understanding these basics will help you better diagnose and fix microphone issues on your iPhone.

Clear sound is essential for many iPhone functions. Imagine trying to have a phone call, but the other person can't hear you well. Or recording a video, but the sound is muffled. This can be very frustrating. Clear sound ensures that your voice is heard clearly during calls, recordings, and when using voice commands with Siri.

Good microphone performance also improves the quality of videos you record. Whether you're capturing a family moment or creating content for social media, clear audio is important. This guide will help you maintain your iPhone's microphone performance so you can always have clear sound.

Chapter 1

Identifying Microphone Problems

Common Symptoms of Microphone Issues

Microphone issues can be frustrating, especially when they disrupt important conversations or recordings. Here are some common symptoms that indicate your iPhone's microphone might be malfunctioning:

1. People Can't Hear You on Calls: If you're on a phone call and the person on the other end cannot hear you clearly, or at all, it could be a sign of a microphone issue. This might happen with regular calls, FaceTime, or any other calling app.

2. Muffled or Distorted Sound: If your voice sounds muffled or distorted to others, it might mean there is something blocking the microphone. Dirt, dust, or even a phone case can sometimes cover the microphone opening and affect the sound quality.

3. No Sound in Recordings: If you record a video or a voice memo and there's no sound or the sound is very faint, it indicates that the microphone might not be capturing audio properly. This problem can be with the front, back, or primary microphone.

4. Intermittent Sound Issues: Sometimes, the microphone might work perfectly at times and not at all at other times. These intermittent issues

can be due to a loose connection inside the phone or temporary blockages.

5. Siri Can't Hear You: If Siri is not responding to your voice commands, it could be due to a microphone issue. Siri relies on the microphone to pick up your voice, and if it can't hear you, it won't be able to process your commands.

6. Background Noise Overpowers Your Voice: If during a call or recording, background noise is louder than your voice, it could be a sign that your microphone isn't functioning correctly. Microphones are built to pick up your voice clearly, even in noisy surroundings.

These symptoms can affect your iPhone's performance in various ways. For example, poor microphone quality can lead to misunderstandings during phone calls, ruined video recordings, and the inability to use voice-activated features like Siri. Identifying these symptoms early can help you take the necessary steps to fix the issue before it becomes more serious.

How to Test Your iPhone Microphones

Testing your iPhone's microphones is a crucial step in identifying and diagnosing microphone problems. Each iPhone typically has three microphones: the primary microphone (located at the bottom of the phone), the front microphone (near the front camera), and the back microphone (near the rear camera). Here are detailed steps on how to test each microphone:

1. Testing the Primary Microphone:

-The iPhone Voice Memos app should be launched.

-Tapping the red record button will start the recording.

-Use the phone's bottom microphone to speak clearly.

. -Tap the red stop button to put an end to recording.

- Playback the recording to see if you can hear your voice clearly.

- If the sound is clear, the primary microphone is working fine. If the sound is faint, muffled, or absent, there might be an issue with the primary microphone.

2. Testing the Front Microphone:

   - Open the Camera app on your iPhone.

   - Switch to the front-facing camera by tapping the camera flip icon.

   - Select the video mode and start recording a short video.

   - Speak clearly towards the front microphone, which is near the front camera.

   - Stop the recording and play back the video in the Photos app.

   - Listen to the audio to check if your voice is clear. If it is, the front microphone is functioning properly. If not, there might be an issue with the front microphone.

3. Testing the Back Microphone:

   - Open the Camera app on your iPhone.

   - Ensure that the back camera is active.

- Select the video mode and start recording a short video.

- Speak clearly towards the back microphone, which is near the rear camera.

- Stop the recording and play back the video in the Photos app.

- Listen to the audio to check if your voice is clear. If it is, the back microphone is working as expected. If not, there might be an issue with the back microphone.

4. Testing the Speakerphone Microphone:
- Give a friend or a family member a call.
- During the call, switch to speakerphone mode. Inquire as to whether the person on the other end can hear you clearly.

- If they can't hear you well, it might indicate a problem with the microphone used for the speakerphone.

5. Testing with Third-Party Apps:

- Open an app like WhatsApp or Skype that uses the microphone for voice and video calls.

- Try making a call or try sending a message.

- Check if the person on the other end can hear you clearly or if the voice message plays back clearly.

- If the audio is not clear, the microphone might not be working properly in that specific app.

6. Testing with Siri

- Activate Siri by holding down the Home button (for older iPhones) or saying "Hey Siri" (for newer iPhones).

- Ask Siri a question or give a command.

- If Siri responds accurately, the microphone is picking up your voice correctly. If not, there might be an issue with the microphone.

By following these steps, you can accurately identify which microphone is having problems. This information is crucial for diagnosing the issue and deciding on the next steps for repair. If you find that a particular microphone is not working, you can proceed with cleaning it or adjusting the settings, as will be discussed in the next chapters of this guide.

Chapter 2

Basic Troubleshooting Steps

Restarting Your iPhone

Restarting your iPhone is one of the simplest yet most effective troubleshooting steps you can take. It helps resolve many minor issues, including those affecting the microphone. When you restart your iPhone, it refreshes the device's software and clears out temporary glitches that might be causing problems.

To restart your iPhone, follow these steps:

1. Turn Off Your iPhone:

- For iPhones with Face ID (iPhone X and later): Press and hold the side button along with either the volume up or volume down button until you see the power-off slider. To switch off your iPhone, drag the slider.

- For iPhones with a Home button (iPhone 8 and earlier): Press and hold the top (or side) button until you see the power-off slider.

2. Turn On Your iPhone:

- Once your iPhone is completely off, press and hold the side button (or the top button for older models) until you see the Apple logo. Release the button and wait for your iPhone to start up.

3. Check the Microphone:

- After your iPhone has restarted, test the microphone again using the steps outlined in

Chapter 1. Record a voice memo or make a call to see if the issue has been resolved.

Checking for Blockages

Your iPhone's microphones are small and can easily get blocked by dirt, dust, or other debris. Blockages can cause muffled or distorted sound and might even stop the microphone from working altogether.

To check for blockages, follow these steps:

1. Inspect the Microphone Openings:
    - Your iPhone has multiple microphones located at different points. Check the bottom of your iPhone near the charging port, the front near the front camera, and the back near the rear camera.

- Look closely at these areas to see if there is any visible dirt, dust, or debris blocking the openings.

2. Clean the Microphone Openings:

- If you see any blockages, gently clean the microphone openings. Use a soft, dry brush, a clean toothpick, or a can of compressed air to remove the debris. Be very careful not to push the debris further into the microphone or damage the delicate components.

- Avoid using liquids or blowing air directly into the microphone openings as this can cause damage.

3. Check for Protective Covers:

- Sometimes, screen protectors, cases, or films can cover the microphone openings and block sound. If you have a screen protector or case on your iPhone, check to see if it's covering any of the microphones.

- Remove the case or screen protector and test the microphone again to see if it makes a difference.

4. Test the Microphone Again:

- After cleaning the microphone openings and removing any obstructions, test the microphone again by recording a voice memo or making a call. If the sound is clearer, the blockage was likely the cause of the problem.

Removing Accessories

Accessories like headphones, Bluetooth devices, and adapters can sometimes interfere with your iPhone's microphone. Removing these accessories can help determine if they are causing the problem. Here's how to troubleshoot microphone issues by removing accessories:

1. Unplug Headphones and Earbuds:

   - If you have headphones or earbuds plugged into your iPhone, unplug them and test the microphone again. Sometimes, the microphone on the headphones might not be working correctly, which can make it seem like the iPhone's microphone is faulty.

2. Disconnect Bluetooth Devices:

   - Your iPhone might be connected to a Bluetooth device that is causing the microphone issue. To disconnect Bluetooth devices, go to Settings > Bluetooth and toggle the Bluetooth switch off. This will disconnect all Bluetooth devices from your iPhone.

- Test the microphone again to see if the issue is resolved.

3. Remove Adapters and Dongles:

- If you are using any adapters or dongles (such as a headphone jack adapter), remove them and test the microphone. These accessories can sometimes cause compatibility issues that affect the microphone.

4. Check for Interference from Other Devices:

- Other electronic devices can sometimes cause interference with your iPhone's microphone. Move your iPhone away from other electronic devices and test the microphone again to see if it makes a difference.

5. Test the Microphone Again:

- After removing all accessories and disconnecting Bluetooth devices, test the microphone again by recording a voice memo or making a call. If the microphone works properly, the issue was likely caused by one of the accessories.

Chapter 3

Cleaning the Microphones

Tools Needed

To clean the microphones on your iPhone properly, you need to have the right tools to do the job safely and effectively. A soft brush, such as a clean, dry paintbrush or a toothbrush, is essential for gently removing dust and debris from the microphone openings without causing any damage. Compressed air is useful for blowing away dust and particles from the microphone openings, but it should be used with short, gentle bursts to avoid damaging the delicate components.

A toothpick or plastic probe can help dislodge any stubborn debris that might be stuck in the microphone openings. It's important to be very gentle with these tools to avoid pushing debris further in or causing damage to the microphone. A lint-free cloth is necessary for wiping around the microphone openings to ensure they are clean and free from any additional dust or dirt. If there is sticky residue or grime around the microphone openings, a small amount of isopropyl alcohol on a lint-free cloth or cotton swab can help clean it. Care should be taken to ensure that no liquid gets into the microphone openings.

Having these tools ready will make the cleaning process easier and more effective. It is crucial to handle your iPhone and the tools gently to avoid causing any damage.

Step-by-Step Cleaning Guide

Cleaning the microphones on your iPhone is a straightforward process, but it requires careful handling to ensure you don't damage the sensitive components. Begin by turning off your iPhone to prevent any accidental damage or triggering of the device during the cleaning process. This can be done by pressing and holding the power button until the power-off slider appears, then dragging the slider to turn off your iPhone.

Next, inspect the microphone openings. The locations of the microphones are typically near the charging port, the front camera and speaker, and the rear camera. Examine these areas closely to see if there is any visible dust, dirt, or debris.

Using a soft brush, gently remove any loose dust or debris from the microphone openings. Brush in a circular motion and avoid pressing too hard to prevent damage. If using a toothbrush, make sure it is clean and dry before use.

Hold the can of compressed air upright and use short, gentle bursts to blow away any remaining dust or particles from the microphone openings. Do not hold the can too close to the iPhone to avoid damaging the microphone. Be careful not to blow air directly into the microphone openings for too long, as this can cause damage. If there is debris that cannot be removed with the brush or compressed air, use a toothpick or plastic probe to carefully dislodge it. Gently insert the toothpick or probe into the microphone opening and move it around to loosen the debris. Avoid pushing the debris further into the microphone and be gentle to prevent any damage to the microphone components.

Use a lint-free cloth to wipe around the microphone openings and remove any additional dust or dirt. This will help ensure that the area is clean and free from debris. If there is sticky residue or grime around the microphone openings, dampen a lint-free cloth or cotton swab with a small amount of isopropyl alcohol. Gently wipe around the microphone openings to clean the area, being careful not to let any liquid get into the microphone openings, as this can cause damage.

After cleaning the microphones, turn your iPhone back on and test the microphone to see if the sound quality has improved. Record a voice memo, make a call, or use an app that requires the microphone to check if the issue has been resolved. By following these steps, you can effectively clean your iPhone's microphones and improve their performance.

Regular cleaning can help prevent future microphone issues and ensure that your iPhone continues to provide clear sound quality. Cleaning the microphones on your iPhone is a simple but important task that helps maintain the sound quality of your device. Using the right tools and following a careful cleaning process can remove dust, dirt, and debris that might be causing microphone issues. Always handle your iPhone and the cleaning tools gently to avoid causing any damage.

Chapter 4

Checking Microphone Permissions

Accessing Privacy Settings

Understanding and managing microphone permissions on your iPhone is important to ensure that your device functions correctly. Microphone permissions determine which apps can use your microphone. Sometimes, the microphone might not work correctly in an app because the permissions are not set properly. In this section, we will go through the steps to access and adjust these settings.

First, unlock your iPhone and find the "Settings" app on your home screen. The icon looks like a set of gray gears. To access the settings menu, tap this symbol. Once you are in the settings menu, you need to scroll down until you see the option labeled "Privacy." Tap on "Privacy" to enter the privacy settings menu. This menu controls many of the permissions for your iPhone, such as location services, contacts, and, most importantly for our purposes, the microphone.

Within the privacy settings, you will see a list of different categories. Look for the option that says "Microphone." Tap on "Microphone" to access the microphone permissions. This will take you to a screen that lists all the apps on your iPhone that have requested access to your microphone.

Enabling Microphone for Apps

Once you are in the microphone settings, you will see a list of apps with small switches next to them. These switches indicate whether the microphone is enabled or disabled for each app. If the switch is green, it means the microphone is enabled for that app. If the switch is gray, it means the microphone is disabled.

It is important to review this list and make sure that the microphone is enabled for the apps you use frequently. For example, if you use apps like WhatsApp, FaceTime, or Zoom for calls, make sure the switches next to these apps are green. If you find an app where the switch is gray and you need to use the microphone with that app, simply tap the switch to turn it green. This action grants the app permission to access your microphone.

Sometimes, you might encounter an app that is not working properly because it does not have the necessary permissions. For instance, if you are trying to use voice recording features in a note-taking app, but the app does not have microphone access, it will not work correctly. To fix this, you need to find the app in the microphone permissions list and turn on the switch.

It's also a good idea to disable microphone access for apps that do not need it. This can help protect your privacy by ensuring that only necessary apps have access to your microphone. If you see an app in the list that you rarely use or do not remember installing, consider turning off the switch next to that app.

Common Issues and Solutions

Sometimes, even after enabling the microphone for an app, you might still face issues. In such cases, there are a few additional steps you can take to troubleshoot the problem. Make sure the app is updated to the most recent version first. Developers often make updates to improve functionality and fix bugs. To check for updates, go to the App Store, tap on your profile icon, and scroll down to see if there are any available updates for your apps. If there are updates available, tap "Update" next to the app.

If updating the app does not solve the problem, try restarting your iPhone. Restarting the device can often resolve temporary software glitches that might be affecting the microphone. To restart your iPhone, press and hold the power button until the "slide to power off" slider appears. The iPhone can be turned off by sliding the slider. After the device is completely off, press and hold the power button again until the Apple logo appears, indicating that the iPhone is restarting.

If the problem persists, you can try reinstalling the app. To do this, locate the app on your home screen, press and hold the app icon until a menu appears, and then tap "Remove App." Confirm that you want to delete the app. After the app is deleted, go to the App Store, search for the app, and reinstall it.

In some cases, the issue might be related to the iOS version on your iPhone. Make sure the most recent version of iOS is installed on your iPhone.. To check for software updates, go to the "Settings" app, tap "General," and then tap

"Software Update." If an update is available, follow the on-screen instructions to download and install it.

Chapter 5

Updating iOS

Why Updating Helps

Updating your iPhone's operating system, known as iOS, is very important for keeping your device running smoothly and securely. iOS is the software that makes your iPhone work, and Apple regularly releases updates to improve it. These updates can fix bugs, add new features, and improve the overall performance of your iPhone. Here's why updating iOS can help:

First, updates often fix bugs and software glitches. Bugs are small errors in the software that can cause your iPhone to behave unexpectedly. For example, a bug might cause your microphone to stop working correctly or make an app crash. When Apple discovers these bugs, they create updates to fix them. By keeping your iPhone updated, you ensure that these bugs are fixed, which can help your iPhone run more smoothly.

Second, updates can improve the security of your iPhone. With each new iOS version, Apple includes security patches to protect your device from viruses and hackers. If you don't update your iPhone, it can become vulnerable to attacks. Hackers are always looking for new ways to break into devices and steal personal information. By installing the latest updates, you can protect your iPhone from these threats and keep your data safe.

Third, updates can also add new features and improve existing ones. For example, a new iOS update might include a redesigned home screen, new emojis, or enhanced camera functions. These new features can make your iPhone more fun and useful. Additionally, updates often improve the performance of existing features, making your iPhone faster and more efficient.

Updating iOS can also improve the compatibility of your iPhone with other devices and apps. As technology evolves, new apps and devices are created that require the latest iOS version to work properly. If you don't update your iPhone, you might not be able to use these new apps and devices. For example, a new game might require the latest iOS version, or a new smartwatch might only work with updated iPhones. By keeping your iPhone updated, you can ensure that it is compatible with the latest technology.

Lastly, updating iOS can extend the life of your iPhone. Over time, Apple optimizes the software to work better with older devices. These optimizations can help your iPhone run more smoothly and prevent it from becoming slow and unresponsive. By regularly updating your iPhone, you can keep it running well for longer, which can save you money by delaying the need to buy a new device.

How to Update Your iPhone

Updating your iPhone is a straightforward process, but it's important to follow the steps carefully to ensure the update is successful. Here's how to update your iPhone:

The first thing you should do is see if an update is available. Unlock your iPhone and launch the "Settings" app to accomplish this. The symbol resembles a series of gray gears. Scroll down to "General" and tap it once you're in the settings menu. Click "Software Update" under General Settings. An update check will be performed on your iPhone. The screen will show an update if one is available. A notification stating, "Your software is up to date," will appear on your iPhone if it has already received an update.

It's a good idea to backup your iPhone before beginning the upgrade. You won't lose your data in this way in the event that the update goes wrong. iTunes or iCloud can be used to create an iPhone backup. Go to the "Settings" app, press on your name at the top, and then tap on "iCloud" to back up using iCloud. After selecting "iCloud Backup" from the drop-down menu, select "Back Up Now." To create an iTunes backup, first connect your iPhone to your computer, then launch iTunes and select the iPhone icon. Select "Back Up Now" after that.

You are prepared to begin the update after your iPhone has been backed up. Ensure that your iPhone is fully charged and linked to a Wi-Fi network. If you want to make sure your iPhone doesn't die in the middle of an update, it's preferable to plug it into a charger. Select "Download and Install" from the software update menu. It will begin downloading the update to your iPhone. Depending on how big the update is and how quickly your internet is connecting, this may take some time.

Your iPhone will prompt you to install the update after the download is finished. Click or tap "Install Now." The installation process will start on your iPhone. Your iPhone will restart during this period, and the screen will display a progress bar and the Apple logo. During this process, do not disconnect your iPhone from the charger or turn it off. It could take a few minutes to install.

Your iPhone will restart once the installation is finished. To unlock your iPhone when it restarts, you'll need to enter your passcode. You'll be walked through a few setup steps by your iPhone, such as logging in with your Apple ID and accepting the terms and conditions. To finish the setup, adhere to the on-screen directions.

Congratulations, your iPhone is now updated! You can go back to the "Settings" app, tap on "General," and then tap on "Software Update" to confirm that your iPhone is running the latest iOS version. You should also check that all your apps are working correctly. If you experience any issues after the update, try restarting your iPhone or contacting Apple Support for assistance.

Updating your iPhone regularly is an important part of maintaining your device. It ensures that your iPhone has the latest features, bug fixes, and security updates. By following the steps outlined in this chapter, you can easily update your iPhone and keep it running smoothly. Remember to check for updates regularly and install them as soon as they are available to get the best performance and security for your iPhone.

Chapter 6

Resetting iPhone Settings

When to Reset

Resetting your iPhone settings can be a useful step when you are experiencing issues that other troubleshooting methods haven't resolved. There are several situations where resetting your iPhone settings might be necessary.

One common reason to reset your settings is when your iPhone is acting unusually slow or apps are crashing frequently. Sometimes, software glitches or conflicts between settings can cause performance problems. Resetting your settings can clear these glitches and restore your iPhone to normal operation.

Another reason to reset your settings is when you are having trouble with specific features. For example, if your Wi-Fi isn't connecting properly, your Bluetooth isn't pairing with devices, or your microphone isn't working correctly, resetting your settings can often fix these issues. This is because resetting can clear out any incorrect or conflicting settings that might be causing the problem.

If you are experiencing problems with your iPhone's battery life, resetting your settings can also help. Sometimes, background processes or incorrect settings can drain your battery faster than usual. Resetting your settings can stop these processes and return your iPhone to normal battery performance.

Resetting your settings can also be helpful if you are having trouble with your iPhone's overall system stability. If your iPhone is freezing, restarting randomly, or displaying error messages, resetting your settings can clear out any software issues that might be causing these problems.

How to Reset Without Losing Data

When you reset your iPhone settings, it's important to do it in a way that won't delete your data. There are two main types of resets: a full factory reset and a settings reset. A full factory reset will erase all your data, including your photos, apps, and personal information. This should only be done if you are selling or giving away your iPhone or if you are experiencing severe issues that can't be fixed any other way.

A settings reset, on the other hand, will only reset your iPhone's settings without deleting your data. This type of reset is usually sufficient to fix most issues and is much safer because you won't lose your important information. Here's how to reset your iPhone settings without losing data:

First, unlock your iPhone and open the "Settings" app. The icon looks like a set of gray gears. Once you are in the settings menu, scroll down and tap on "General." In the general settings menu, scroll down to the bottom and tap on "Reset."

In the reset menu, you will see several options. To reset your settings without losing data, tap on "Reset All Settings." You might be prompted to enter your passcode. After entering your passcode, you will see a confirmation message asking if you want to reset all settings. Tap on "Reset All Settings" again to confirm.

Your iPhone will start the reset process, which can take a few minutes. During this time, your iPhone will restart, and you will see the Apple logo on the screen. Do not turn off your iPhone or disconnect it from power during this process.

Once the reset is complete, your iPhone will restart again. After it restarts, you will need to enter your passcode to unlock your iPhone. Your settings will be reset to their default values, but your data will remain intact. This means that your photos, apps, and personal information will not be deleted.

After resetting your settings, you might need to reconfigure some settings. For example, you will need to reconnect to Wi-Fi networks, re-pair Bluetooth devices, and re-enter any custom settings you had previously configured. This can take some time, but it is a necessary step to ensure your iPhone is set up correctly.

It's also a good idea to check that all your apps are working correctly after the reset. If you experience any issues with specific apps, try restarting your iPhone or reinstalling the affected apps. If you are still having trouble, you can contact the app developer for assistance.

Resetting your iPhone settings can be a helpful step in resolving various issues, but it's important to do it carefully to avoid losing your data. By following the steps outlined in this chapter, you can reset your settings safely and get your iPhone back to normal operation. Remember to back up your iPhone regularly to protect your data, and only perform a full factory reset if absolutely necessary.

Chapter 7

Advanced Troubleshooting

Testing Microphones Individually

When basic troubleshooting steps don't fix the problem, you might need to test each microphone on your iPhone individually. iPhones have multiple microphones located in different parts of the device. There is usually one at the bottom near the charging port, one at the top near the front camera, and one on the back near the rear camera. Testing each microphone can help identify which one is causing the issue.

To begin, find a quiet place to conduct the tests. Background noise can interfere with your ability to determine if the microphones are working properly. Once you're in a quiet environment, you can start testing each microphone using specific apps on your iPhone.

To test the bottom microphone, which is primarily used for phone calls and voice memos, open the Voice Memos app on your iPhone. This app looks like a white icon with a red recording wave. Once the app is open, tap the record button, which looks like a red circle. Speak clearly into the bottom of your iPhone for about ten seconds. After you finish speaking, tap the stop button, which looks like a red square. Playback the recording to see if you can hear your voice clearly. If the sound is clear, the bottom microphone is working properly. If it's not, you might have found the source of the problem.

Next, test the top microphone, which is used for FaceTime calls and video recordings with the front camera. Open the Camera app on your iPhone. The Camera app icon looks like a gray camera. Switch to the front-facing camera by tapping the camera flip button, which looks like two arrows forming a circle. Record a short video while speaking into the top of your iPhone. After recording, play back the video and listen to the audio. If you can hear your voice clearly, the top microphone is working fine. If not, this microphone might be the issue.

Finally, test the rear microphone, which is used for video recordings with the rear camera. Stay in the Camera app, but switch to the rear camera by tapping the camera flip button again. Record another short video, but this time, speak into the back of your iPhone. Playback the video and listen to the audio. If your voice is clear, the rear microphone is functioning correctly. If the audio is unclear or missing, the rear microphone might be the problem.

By testing each microphone individually, you can pinpoint which one is not working correctly. This information is crucial for determining the next steps in fixing your iPhone's microphone issues.

Using Voice Memos and Camera Apps

The Voice Memos and Camera apps are essential tools for testing your iPhone's microphones and diagnosing problems. These apps are built into every iPhone, making them convenient and easy to use for troubleshooting.

The Voice Memos app is designed for recording audio, making it perfect for testing the bottom microphone. To use this app for troubleshooting, open the Voice Memos app. If you can't find it, swipe down on your home screen and type "Voice Memos" in the search bar.

Once the app is open, tap the red record button. This starts the recording process. Hold your iPhone as you normally would during a phone call and speak into the bottom of the device. Say something like, "Testing, one, two, three." After recording for about ten seconds, tap the stop button. Playback the recording by tapping the play button and listen carefully to the audio. If you hear your voice clearly, the bottom microphone is working. If the sound is faint, distorted, or absent, there might be an issue with the bottom microphone.

The Camera app can test both the top and rear microphones through video recordings. To use it for troubleshooting, open the Camera app. If you can't find it, swipe down on your home screen and type "Camera" in the search bar. Switch to the front-facing camera by tapping the camera flip button. This allows you to test the top microphone. Record a short video by tapping the red record button and speak into the top of your iPhone while recording. After about ten seconds, stop the recording by tapping the red button again. Playback the video and listen to the audio. If you can hear your voice clearly, the top microphone is working. If not, there might be an issue with the top microphone.

Switch to the rear camera by tapping the camera flip button again. This allows you to test the rear microphone. Record another short video, this time speaking into the back of your iPhone. After about ten seconds, stop the recording and play back the video. Listen to the audio to determine if the rear microphone is working properly.

Using these apps, you can systematically test each microphone and gather important information about their functionality. If one of the microphones is not working, you can focus on troubleshooting that specific part of your iPhone.

If the tests indicate that one or more microphones are not working, consider the following steps. Restart your iPhone and repeat the tests to see if the problem persists. Sometimes, a simple restart can fix software-related issues. Check for blockages in the microphone openings. Dust, dirt, or debris can block the microphones and affect their performance. Use a soft, dry brush to gently clean the openings. Remove any accessories, such as cases or screen protectors, that might be covering the microphones. Test the microphones again with the accessories removed.

If these steps don't resolve the issue, you might need to seek professional help. For more help, get in touch with Apple Support or go to one of the approved service providers. They can perform more advanced diagnostics and repairs if necessary.

Chapter 8

Replacing the Microphone

Note: For this Chapter it is advised you allow a Professional handle it. This requires an expert to fix. I only added this Just to enhance the Quality of this Guide. But if you feel you would love to give it a try,Fine. But Note that the author will not be Responsible for any damage Caused during the trying process.

Tools and Materials Needed

Replacing the microphone on an iPhone requires specific tools and materials to ensure a safe and effective repair. It's important to gather all the necessary items before starting the replacement process. Here's a detailed explanation of what you'll need and why each item is essential.

First, you need a replacement microphone that is compatible with your specific iPhone model. Each iPhone model has a different design, so the microphone for an iPhone 7 may not fit an iPhone 11. You can purchase a replacement microphone from electronics stores, online retailers, or specialized repair shops.

Next, you'll need a precision screwdriver set. This set usually includes various screwdriver heads, such as Phillips and Pentalobe, which are essential for removing the tiny screws that hold your iPhone together. iPhones use different screw types in various parts, so having a set with multiple heads ensures you can handle all screws.

Plastic opening tools are also necessary. These tools help you gently pry open the iPhone's casing without causing damage. Using metal tools can scratch or dent the casing, so plastic ones are preferable. They come in different shapes and sizes to help you open the casing from different angles.

Tweezers are useful for handling small components inside the iPhone. They allow you to carefully pick up and place the new microphone without touching it directly with your fingers. This is important because oils and dirt from your hands can damage delicate electronic parts.

Adhesive strips or glue may be needed if your iPhone uses adhesive to hold parts in place.

Some iPhone models have components that are glued down, and you'll need to reapply adhesive to secure them properly after replacing the microphone. Make sure you use adhesives that are designed for electronics to avoid any damage.

Finally, a clean, well-lit workspace is crucial. Replacing an iPhone microphone involves working with very small parts, so having a clear, organized space helps you keep track of all components and tools. Good lighting ensures you can see what you're doing clearly, reducing the risk of making mistakes.

Step-by-Step Replacement Guide

Now that you have all the necessary tools and materials, it's time to replace the microphone.

Follow these detailed steps to ensure a successful replacement.

First, power off your iPhone to prevent any electrical issues. Hold down the power button until the "slide to power off" option appears, then slide to turn off the device. Once your iPhone is off, remove any accessories like cases or screen protectors.

Next, use the precision screwdriver to remove the screws at the bottom of the iPhone near the charging port. These screws are usually Pentalobe screws, so use the appropriate head from your screwdriver set. Keep the screws in a safe place where they won't get lost.

With the screws removed, use a plastic opening tool to gently pry open the iPhone's casing. Start at the bottom and work your way around the edges, carefully separating the casing without bending or cracking it. In order to prevent breaking the casing, take your time and use light pressure.

Once the casing is open, you'll see the internal components of your iPhone. Locate the battery connector and use the plastic opening tool to disconnect it. This step ensures there is no power running through the device while you're working on it, preventing short circuits.

Locate the old microphone, which is usually near the bottom of the iPhone close to the charging port. Use tweezers to carefully remove the old microphone from its housing. Note how it is positioned, as you'll need to install the new microphone in the same way.

Take the new microphone and place it into the housing, ensuring it fits securely and is oriented correctly. If your iPhone uses adhesive to hold the microphone in place, apply the adhesive before positioning the new microphone. Make sure the adhesive doesn't cover any important contacts or parts.

Reconnect the battery by pressing the connector back into place with the plastic opening tool. Ensure it is securely connected, as a loose connection can cause your iPhone not to power on or function correctly.

Before closing the casing, power on your iPhone to test the new microphone. Press and hold the power button until the Apple logo shows. Once your iPhone is on, make a test call or record an audio clip using the Voice Memos app to check if the new microphone works correctly. Speak clearly into the microphone and play back the recording to ensure the sound is clear.

If the microphone works well, power off your iPhone again. Carefully close the casing by pressing the edges together until they snap into place. Make sure all sides are aligned and the casing is securely closed. Finally, use the precision screwdriver to reinsert and tighten the screws you removed earlier.

Perform a final test of the microphone to confirm everything is working correctly. Make another call or record an audio clip to ensure the sound is clear and there are no issues with the new microphone.

Replacing the microphone on your iPhone can be a delicate process, but with the right tools, materials, and careful attention to detail, you can successfully complete the repair. If at any point you feel unsure or encounter difficulties, it's always a good idea to seek professional help from Apple or an authorized service provider. This ensures the repair is done correctly and safely, protecting your iPhone from further damage.

Chapter 9

When to Seek Professional Help

Recognizing When DIY Isn't Enough

Repairing your iPhone microphone by yourself can be a rewarding experience. However, there are times when do-it-yourself (DIY) solutions may not be enough. Knowing when to seek professional help is important to avoid causing further damage to your device.

One sign that you might need professional help is if you've tried all basic troubleshooting steps and the problem persists. For example, if you have restarted your iPhone, checked for blockages, removed accessories, cleaned the microphones, checked microphone permissions, updated iOS, reset settings, and even replaced the microphone, but the issue is still there, it is a clear indication that you need expert assistance.

Another sign is if you encounter complex issues beyond your technical skills. iPhones are sophisticated devices with many tiny and delicate components. If you accidentally damage another part while trying to fix the microphone, it can cause more problems. For instance, if you break a connector, tear a ribbon cable, or damage the logic board, the repair becomes much more complicated and expensive. In such cases, seeking professional help is the best option to ensure your iPhone is fixed correctly.

Also, if your iPhone is still under warranty, it's wise to let professionals handle the repair. Apple provides a one-year limited warranty for new iPhones and an extended warranty if you have AppleCare+. Attempting to repair your iPhone on your own can void the warranty, meaning you might have to pay for any future repairs out of pocket. By contacting Apple or an authorized service provider, you can ensure the repair is covered under warranty and performed by qualified technicians.

If you experience hardware-related issues, such as a damaged logic board or other internal components, professional help is necessary. These types of repairs require specialized tools and expertise that most people don't have. Trying to fix such issues on your own can result in permanent damage to your iPhone.

Lastly, if you are unsure about any step in the repair process, it's better to seek help. Uncertainty can lead to mistakes that might worsen the problem. Professional technicians have the training and experience to diagnose and fix issues accurately and efficiently.

How to Contact Apple Support

When you decide that it's time to seek professional help for your iPhone microphone problem, contacting Apple Support is the best course of action. Apple Support offers several ways to get assistance, ensuring you receive the help you need in a convenient manner.

The easiest way to contact Apple Support is through their official website. Visit **[support.apple.com](https://support.apple.co**

m) and navigate to the iPhone section. Here, you can find troubleshooting articles, guides, and videos that might help you resolve the issue on your own. If you still need assistance, you can initiate a support request online.

To start a support request, click on the "Get Support" button on the Apple Support website. You'll need to enter your Apple ID to log in.. Once signed in, you can describe the issue you're experiencing with your iPhone microphone. Apple Support will provide you with options to either chat with a support representative, schedule a call, or book an appointment at an Apple Store or authorized service provider.

Another convenient way to contact Apple Support is through the Apple Support app, which you can download from the App Store. The app provides access to a wide range of support resources and allows you to connect with support representatives directly. You can also track the status of your repair and find information about warranty coverage.

If you prefer speaking with a support representative over the phone, you can call Apple Support directly. The phone number for Apple Support varies by country and region, so you'll need to check the Apple Support website for the correct number for your location. When you call, be prepared to provide details about your iPhone model, the issue you're experiencing, and any troubleshooting steps you've already taken.

For those who live near an Apple Store or an authorized service provider, booking an appointment for an in-person visit is an excellent option. To do this, go to the Apple Support website or use the Apple Support app to schedule a visit. During your appointment, a technician will diagnose the problem and discuss repair options with you. In many cases, repairs can be completed on-site while you wait.

If your iPhone requires service, Apple offers mail-in repair options. After contacting Apple Support and describing the issue, they may suggest mailing your device to an Apple Repair Center. Apple will provide you with shipping instructions and a prepaid shipping label. Once the repair is complete, your iPhone will be shipped back to you. This option is convenient if you don't have an Apple Store or authorized service provider nearby.

In addition to Apple's own support services, you can also seek help from Apple Authorized Service Providers (AASPs). AASPs are independent companies that have been authorized by Apple to perform repairs on Apple products. They use genuine Apple parts and follow Apple's repair guidelines, ensuring high-quality service. You can find an AASP near you by visiting the Apple Support website and using the service provider locator tool.

Before submitting your iPhone to an Apple Repair Center or having it repaired, be sure you have a backup of the device. By backing up your data, you can be sure that during the repair procedure, you don't lose any crucial information. You may backup your iPhone using iCloud or iTunes.. To create an iCloud backup, select "Backup Now" after going to Settings > [your name] > iCloud > iCloud Backup. Connect your iPhone to your computer, launch iTunes, choose your device, and then click "Back Up Now" to create an iTunes backup.

Chapter 10

Preventive Maintenance

Tips to Keep Your Microphone Working

Maintaining the microphone on your iPhone is essential for ensuring that it functions properly. A well-maintained microphone will provide clear sound during calls, recordings, and other uses. There are several tips you can follow to keep your microphone in good condition.

First, protect your iPhone from physical damage. Using a sturdy case can help prevent your phone from getting damaged if it falls. A damaged iPhone can lead to internal problems, including microphone issues. Make sure to choose a case that provides good protection without blocking the microphone openings.

Keep your iPhone away from moisture. Water and electronics do not mix well. If your iPhone gets wet, it can cause serious damage to the internal components, including the microphone. Avoid using your phone in places where it might get wet, like in the rain or near a pool. **If your iPhone does get wet, dry it off immediately and avoid turning it on until you are sure it is completely dry.**

Avoid exposing your iPhone to extreme temperatures. Both high and low temperatures can affect the performance of your phone. **High temperatures can cause the internal components to expand and contract, which can lead to damage. Cold temperatures can**

cause the battery to drain faster and affect the overall performance of your phone. Try to keep your iPhone in a moderate temperature environment as much as possible.

Regularly update your iPhone's software. Apple releases updates that often include fixes for known issues, including problems with the microphone. Keeping your iPhone's software up to date can help prevent problems before they occur. To check for updates, go to Settings, then General, and then Software Update.

Be mindful of how you hold your iPhone. When making a call or recording audio, make sure your hand or fingers are not covering the microphone openings. Blocking the microphone can muffle the sound and make it difficult for others to hear you clearly.

Use only genuine Apple accessories. **Using non-Apple chargers, cables, or other accessories can sometimes cause problems with your iPhone, including microphone issues.** Genuine Apple accessories are designed to work perfectly with your iPhone and can help prevent potential issues.

If you use headphones with a built-in microphone, make sure they are in good condition. Broken or damaged headphones can cause problems with sound quality. Inspect your headphones regularly for any signs of wear and tear, and replace them if necessary.

Be careful with third-party apps. Some apps can interfere with your iPhone's microphone settings. If you notice microphone issues after installing a new app, try uninstalling the app to see if the problem goes away. Only download apps from trusted sources and be cautious of granting microphone access to apps that do not need it.

Regular Cleaning and Care

Regular cleaning and care of your iPhone's microphone can help maintain its performance and extend its lifespan. Over time, dirt, dust, and debris can accumulate in the microphone openings, causing sound quality to degrade. Here are some steps you can follow to keep your microphone clean and well-maintained although I have said these countlessly.

Use a soft, dry brush to gently clean the microphone openings. A small, clean paintbrush or a toothbrush with soft bristles works well for this purpose. Gently brush the microphone openings to remove any dust or debris. Avoid using too much pressure, as this can push debris further into the openings.

For more stubborn dirt, you can use a can of compressed air. Hold the can upright and spray short bursts of air into the microphone openings. Be careful not to hold the can too close to the openings, as the force of the air can damage the internal components. Using compressed air can help dislodge any debris that is stuck inside the microphone.

If you prefer not to use compressed air, you can also use a small piece of adhesive tape. Gently press the sticky side of the tape over the microphone openings and then lift it away. The tape can help pull out any dirt or dust that is stuck inside. Make sure to use a tape that is not too sticky, as you do not want to leave any residue behind.

Avoid using liquid cleaners or blowing into the microphone openings with your mouth. Liquid cleaners can seep into the internal components and cause damage. Blowing into the openings with your mouth can introduce moisture, which can also cause problems.

After cleaning, inspect the microphone openings to make sure they are clear. If the openings still appear dirty, repeat the cleaning process.

Regularly check your iPhone's case and screen protector for any signs of wear and tear. Cases and screen protectors can collect dust and dirt over time, which can end up blocking the microphone openings. Clean your case and screen protector regularly to prevent this from happening.

It's also important to handle your iPhone with clean hands. Oils and dirt from your hands can transfer to your phone, including the microphone openings. Washing your hands before using your iPhone can help keep it clean.

Store your iPhone in a clean, dry place when not in use. Keeping your phone in a dusty or dirty environment can lead to the buildup of debris in the microphone openings. Use a protective case or pouch to keep your iPhone safe when you're not using it.

If you use your iPhone in a dusty or dirty environment, consider using a protective cover that includes dust filters. These covers can help prevent dust and dirt from entering the microphone openings while still allowing sound to pass through.

Conclusion

In this guide, we have covered various aspects of identifying, troubleshooting, and repairing iPhone microphone issues. Let's summarize the key points we've discussed throughout the chapters.

We started by identifying common microphone problems. These issues include muffled or unclear sound, people not being able to hear you on calls, and the microphone not working in specific apps. Recognizing these symptoms is the first step in diagnosing the problem.

Next, we explored basic troubleshooting steps. These steps include restarting your iPhone, checking for blockages in the microphone openings, and removing any accessories that might interfere with the microphone's functionality. These simple actions can often resolve minor issues and improve the microphone's performance.

Cleaning the microphones is an essential maintenance task. We discussed the tools needed for cleaning, such as a soft brush, compressed air, and a microfiber cloth. A detailed step-by-step cleaning guide helps you clean your microphone safely without causing any damage.

Checking microphone permissions is crucial when your microphone doesn't work in certain apps. We explained how to access privacy settings and ensure that the microphone is enabled for the required apps. This step ensures that the apps can use the microphone properly.

Updating your iPhone's iOS can fix many software-related microphone issues. We covered why keeping your iOS up-to-date is important and provided a guide on how to update your iPhone. Regular updates ensure that your device runs smoothly and that any known bugs affecting the microphone are addressed.

Resetting iPhone settings can help resolve persistent microphone problems without losing your data. We discussed when to reset your iPhone settings and how to do it safely. This action can restore the microphone to its default settings and fix any configuration issues.

Advanced troubleshooting involves testing each microphone individually using the Voice Memos and Camera apps. By doing this, you can identify which specific microphone is causing the problem. This step is crucial in diagnosing hardware issues that might require further action.

For those willing to undertake a more challenging task, we provided a comprehensive guide on replacing the microphone. We detailed the tools and materials needed and offered a step-by-step replacement guide. This information is helpful for DIY enthusiasts who feel confident in their repair skills although it is advisable you seek the help of a Professional on that.

Knowing when to seek professional help is vital. We discussed recognizing when DIY efforts aren't enough and provided information on how to contact Apple Support. Sometimes, professional intervention is necessary to fix complex hardware issues.

Preventive maintenance is the key to keeping your iPhone's microphone in good working condition. We shared tips on regular cleaning and care to avoid future problems. By following these practices, you can extend the lifespan of your microphone and ensure its optimal performance.

This guide has equipped you with the knowledge and steps to troubleshoot and repair your iPhone's microphone. By following the steps and tips provided, you can confidently address microphone issues and maintain your device's functionality. Embrace your DIY spirit, learn from your experiences, and continue to grow your skills. Happy repairing!